FEB 2 1 2011

8-17(3)

D1126937

Delaware

BY MARI KESSELRING

The Child's World

Published by The Child's World®
1980 Lookout Drive • Mankato, MN 56003-1705
800-599-READ • www.childsworld.com

ACKNOWLEDGMENTS
The Child's World®: Mary Berendes, Publishing Director
The Design Lab: Design and production
Red Line Editorial: Editorial direction

PHOTO CREDITS: C Minus Images, LLC/iStockphoto, cover, 1, 3; Matt Kania/
Map Hero, Inc., 4, 5; Johnny Stockshooter/Photolibrary, 7; Elisa Frank/
iStockphoto, 9; College of Agriculture and Natural Resources at the University
of Delaware, 10; Nancy Nehring/iStockphoto, 11; Teresa Levite/Bigstock, 13;
Photolibrary, 15; David Kay/Shutterstock Images, 17; Manuel Balce Ceneta/
AP Images, 19; iStockphoto, 21; One Mile Up, 22; Quarter-dollar coin image
from the United States Mint, 22

LIBRARY OF CONGRESS CATALOGING-IN-PUBLICATION DATA
Kesselring, Mari.
  Delaware / by Mari Kesselring.
      p. cm.
  Includes bibliograpical references and index.
  ISBN 978-1-60253-452-0 (library bound : alk. paper)
  1. Delaware—Juvenile literature. I. Title.

F164.3.K47 2010
975.1—dc22

                                        2010017672

Printed in the United States of America in Mankato, Minnesota.
July 2010
F11538

On the cover: The Harbor of Refuge **Lighthouse** in Lewes, Delaware, was built in 1926.

CONTENTS

Geography

Let's explore Delaware! Delaware is in the northeastern United States. Its eastern border is the Delaware Bay and the Atlantic Ocean. Delaware is the second-smallest state.

PENNSYLVANIA

• Greenville

• Wilmington

• Newark

• New Castle

NEW JERSEY

Delaware River

DELAWARE

• Smyrna

Dover ⭐

MARYLAND

• Felton

Delaware Bay

Harrington • • Milford

• Bridgeville

Georgetown •

• Lewes

• Rehoboth Beach

Atlantic Ocean

• Millsboro

Laurel •

• Fenwick Island

NORTH

WEST — EAST

SOUTH

Cities

Dover is the capital of Delaware.
Wilmington is the state's largest city.
Newark is another large city.

Wilmington is home to about 70,000 people. ▶

Land

Delaware has low **marshes** and sandy beaches. The Delaware River creates the border between Delaware and New Jersey. Higher areas of land are along the riverbanks.

Although Rehoboth Beach is a **popular** place to visit, ▶ some parts of the beach are undisturbed by people.

Plants and Animals

Forests cover part of Delaware. The Delaware state tree is the American holly. Many birds and flowers are found in the state. The state bird is the blue hen. The state flower is the peach blossom.

Peach blossoms are the flowers of peach trees. ▶

People and Work

More than 850,000 people live in Delaware. Some people work as farmers. Chicken farms are common. **Manufacturing** is important to the state. Delaware has many companies that make **chemicals**.

A ship carries coal on a waterway in Delaware. ▶

History

Several Native American **tribes** have lived in the Delaware area for thousands of years. People from Europe came to the area in the 1600s. Delaware became a **colony** owned by England. Americans gained their freedom from England during the **American Revolution**. Delaware became the first U.S. state on December 7, 1787.

General George Washington, who became the first president of the United States, crossed the Delaware ▶ River with his men during the American Revolution.

Delaware is nicknamed "the First State."

Ways of Life

People in Delaware enjoy visiting the state's many beaches. They can fish and ride in boats. The Delaware State Fair is a popular event. It is held every year in Harrington.

Two men fish on a Delaware beach at sunset. ▶

Famous People

Joe Biden was a senator from Delaware for 36 years. In 2009, he became vice president of the United States. Inventor Henry Heimlich was born in Delaware. He invented a way to save people from choking.

Vice President Joe Biden speaks to audiences around the country. ▶

Famous Places

Delaware has many **museums**. The Delaware History Museum in Wilmington helps visitors learn about the rich history of the state. Delaware has large, old **libraries** to visit, too. Some buildings in Delaware are more than 200 years old.

Winterthur is an old home and museum in Delaware that has large gardens. ▶

State Symbols

Seal

The Delaware state seal has pictures of a **soldier** and a farmer. Go to childsworld.com/links for a link to Delaware's state Web site, where you can get a firsthand look at the state seal.

Flag

The ribbon on the Delaware state flag shows the state's **motto**, "Liberty and Independence."

Quarter

Caesar Rodney is on the Delaware state quarter. He spoke up for Delaware when the United States was forming. The quarter came out in 1999.

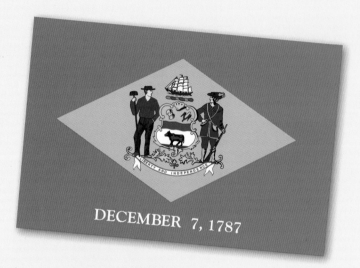

DECEMBER 7, 1787

Glossary

American Revolution (uh-MER-ih-kin rev-uh-LOO-shun): During the American Revolution, from 1775 to 1783, the 13 American colonies fought against Britain for their independence. People in Delaware fought in the American Revolution.

chemicals (KEM-uh-kulz): Chemicals are substances used in chemistry. Some companies in Delaware make chemicals.

colony (KOL-uh-nee): A colony is an area of land that is newly settled and is controlled by a government of another land. Delaware was once a colony owned by England.

libraries (LY-brayr-eez): Libraries are places where books, magazines, and other items can be borrowed. Delaware has libraries that are very old.

lighthouse (LYT-howss): A lighthouse is a tall building near an ocean or large lake that uses lights to warn ships of danger. The Harbor of Refuge Lighthouse is in Lewes, Delaware.

manufacturing (man-yuh-FAK-chur-ing): Manufacturing is the task of making items with machines. Many people in Delaware work in manufacturing.

marshes (MARSH-ez): Marshes are wet, low lands. Delaware has marshes.

motto (MOT-oh): A motto is a sentence that states what people stand for or believe. Delaware's motto is "Liberty and Independence."

museums (myoo-ZEE-umz): Museums are places where people go to see art, history, or science displays. Delaware has museums.

popular (POP-yuh-lur): To be popular is to be enjoyed by many people. The Delaware State Fair is a popular event.

seal (SEEL): A seal is a symbol a state uses for government business. A farmer is on Delaware's seal.

soldier (SOHL-jur): A soldier is a person who is in the army. A soldier is on Delaware's seal.

symbols (SIM-bulz): Symbols are pictures or things that stand for something else. The state seal and flag are Delaware's symbols.

tribes (TRYBZ): Tribes are groups of people who share ancestors and customs. Native American tribes live in Delaware.

Further Information

Books

Crane, Carol. *F is for First State: A Delaware Alphabet*. Chelsea, MI: Sleeping Bear Press, 2004.

Keller, Laurie. *The Scrambled States of America*. New York: Henry Holt, 2002.

Wolny, Philip. *Delaware: Past and Present*. New York: Rosen Central, 2010.

Web Sites

Visit our Web site for links about Delaware: *childsworld.com/links*

Note to Parents, Teachers, and Librarians: We routinely verify our Web links to make sure they are safe and active sites. So encourage your readers to check them out!

Index